Kingdoms of Silence

James Waller (b.1978) is an Australian born artist and poet of mixed Maltese, English and Irish ancestry. He studied Visual Arts at Sydney College of the Arts, Newcastle University and the Malmö Art Academy, and Art History at the University of Melbourne. He has been a featured poet in numerous events in Melbourne, Brisbane and Dublin, including Passionate Tongues, The Dan Poetry readings, The Courthouse readings, The Spinning Room (Melbourne), Speed Poets (Brisbane), Brown Bread Mix Tape (Dublin) and the Clonakilty Arts Festival (Clonakilty, Ireland).

A full time artist and writer, he lives in Clonakilty, Ireland, where he runs the Clonakilty School of Painting, teaching classical painting, drawing and printmaking to children and adults. *Kingdoms of Silence* collates his fourth, fifth and sixth collections of poetry written between 2005 - 2008. For more of his work visit: www.jameswaller.org

Kingdoms of Silence

James Waller

Poems Vol. II

ISBN: 9798362189358
Independently published
Typeset in Athelas

Cover image: *Sea of Time and Room Enough*, oil and mixed media on
canvas (detail), 2014-15, by Michael McSwiney.
Reproduced with permission.

Acknowledgements

Your Voice and *Melbourne Drifts* were first published in Five Poetry
Journal, *Swedish Runes* in Eureka Street, *The Photograph* in Stylus Poetry
Journal. A reading of *Prisoners of Silence* was screened on Channel 31
(Melbourne). An audio recording of *The Call* was broadcast on 3RRR
(Melbourne independent radio).
Many of these poems have been read at poetry gigs in Melbourne,
Dublin and Clonakilty. A big thank you to the conveners and to the
vibrant poetry community in Melbourne, which provided the first
space for these poems to emerge.
The epigraph is taken from *A Draft of Shadows*, in 'The Collected
Poems of Octavio Paz', translated by Eliot Weinberger
for New Directions, 1991.
A special thank you to Michael McSwiney for the cover image, and
to Sheila, as always, for her love and support.

Contents

II. The Invisible Nation 67

III. Night Palace 129

Illustrations
Oil paintings by the author, reproduced in b&w

Introduction

By the beginning of August in 1997 I had made my way to Paris, after one month traveling in Scandinavia, and one month in England, the land of my father's forebears. I was on a summer journey, between semesters at the Malmö Art Academy in Sweden, where I was studying for one year on a university exchange program. One fine afternoon in Paris I found myself transfixed at the entrance to the Musée National d'Art Moderne. There, on the entrance wall hung 'The Sorrow of the King', created by Henri Matisse in 1952. It is, I believe, Matisse's greatest work; his 'swan song', the most resonant pulsation of his inner chromatic fire, forged, or yielded, two years before his passing from the world.

The blues and golds of Matisse flood the first part of this volume. 'Kingdoms of Silence' is (for me) as deep and serenely balanced, as 'Blinded Bulls' (part three of 'Insomnia's Gates') is fierce and meteoric. After the dark ferocity of 'the bulls' I needed the deep lakes of stillness, and the fresh leaves of celebration which emerge in the gentle light of spring and the sparkling pageants of autumn. I needed this stillness to calm a nervous system devastated by the ferocity of my lyrical anger against the savagery of people against people. I was compelled to restore balance to my mind and soul.

Still the anger remained and remains. 'Porcelain', 'Death Rows', and 'The Prince' are the most resonant manifestations. But they are quiet in metre, calm in rhythm, and to my mind are all the more deadly for it!

What has saved me from sinking into 'moral rage' is a newfound awareness of the 'empty light of illusion', lyrically questioned and realized in the strange poem "Bitch Jazz". In this poem the persona of the 'onyx', an imaginary wild cat, is affirmed as the new voice of the poet.

The onyx is a shamelessly Borgesian creature who, whilst born of empathy and wonder, is also a player of the mysterious games of art, hovering above the Balthusian coloured chess board in the gentle breeze of aesthetic delight. This is not formalism, but surrender to the magical speech of the Muse.

Where 'Kingdoms of Silence' is marked by healing and enchantment, 'The Invisible Nation', which follows, is torched by the searing heat of injustice and the cruelty of the state.

At the heart of 'The Invisible Nation' are ballads for the stateless and the disposessed, for the 'lost songs', for the 'prisoners of silence'. These poems were written at a time when the Australian government was incarcerating asylum seekers who had arrived by boat from Indonesia, in the Baxter Detention Centre, in the South Australian desert. Protesters would bus to what was essentially a prison for those fleeing repression, to protest against a heartless governmental policy.

These protests prompted three of the central poems in this collection: 'The Invisible Nation', 'The Crucifix of Silence' and 'Speech is a Tongue of Branches'; they represent my own lyrical protest against the Australian government's immoral treatment of those persecuted individuals seeking our aid.

Following the balladic rage of these central pieces, the collection settles into a mood of reflective elegy and, finally, into a profound meditation on something called 'the chamber', which prefigures the great spiritual awakening in 'The Call', the culmination of 'Night Palace', the third part of this volume.

The poetic 'voice' in 'Night Palace' has a disturbing 'beyond the grave' quality about it. The strange one-line poem 'The Carpet of the Living' sets an other-worldly tone, as if a spirit is silently observing the world of 'the living'. Moreover, the voice addresses the reader as if they, too, are a spirit.

As a poet I have learned to accept the 'voice' in whatever form it takes. As incomprehensible, yet compelling lines unfurl I go with the music, allowing the image to eventually reveal its treasure. This 'treasure' may itself be a riddle; but it invariably glows with a sense of completeness and truthfulness that I cannot ignore.

Sometimes, however, the words are so strange, that I delete them, only for them to return, insisting on being. On one occasion, in a poem called 'Balance the Roses', I allowed this feeling of bewilderment to become part of the poem:

Balance the roses. What is that? Balance the roses. Again, what is that? Twins balance roses in the darkness. In the mirrors, in the darkness...

Sometime after the completion of this poem I understood its significance, but at the time I wrote it, or allowed itself to unfurl, I was as bewildered by it as the reader no doubt is (or perhaps it makes perfect sense, who am I to say?)!

Although 'Night Palace' culminates in 'The Call', 'The Call' was written well before and was never really an organic part of the collection. The poems in 'Night Palace' were in some ways contrived to reignite a poetic space I had already conjured, or in some ways to imagine the space of the 'chamber' that the author enters in 'The Call'. Of this poem I will say nothing, except that it is probably the most important poem I have written.

The reach of poetry is mysterious and the poet can only unfurl what is within them, trusting that in someone, somewhere their work will touch a chord, brighten nervature, enflame a response.

As the inventor of the hologram, Hans Weil, told me one wintry afternoon in 1997, "language is the anonymous masterpiece". May we all grow from its rich and mysterious well.

James Waller, 2005-2022

*for the pilgrims, and for the prisoners;
may you find courage and solace
in "the temple of the preacher"*

*

*"I write because the druid,
under the murmuring syllables of the hymn,
ilex planted deeply on the page,
gave me the branch of mistletoe, the spell
that makes words flow from stone."*

Octavio Paz
(trans. Eliot Weinberger)

I
Kingdoms of Silence

Poem

A bench and a tree
What more could you want?

Deck

Scrapes,
Rolling sounds,
Horns and distant lines;
An invisible bird
Underscores the hint
Of a siren
And a prescription of rubber
Medicates the road -
The poor suffering road,
It's blistered limb.
We are waiting,
All are waiting
In the conference of the roads
Where speech is the morse code
Of the earth hammer, the Jack
Whose anonymous card
Is played
Without repose
Or foresight
For the consequences.
Move over!
Let me deal a hand
But can you cut the cards?

Out of Tune

The corridors are singing
Out of tune
The banshee's scream is gone.
Feet strike the floor
In staccato punch,
A rhyme feathers to the ground
Out of time with sound.
Drinks clink
From a hidden fridge
All is calm.
The pen sits in a fragile case
Of dismembered ink
Books are lined with fires
Concealed
In their paper ribs
More redolent than bone.
Hum mighty ones, fridges of the night
And the endless day;
The news has recovered
From the shock of its revealed mask
And the air is thin
As February's streaming hair
Blasting
Through tired eyes
And whipping the corridor
Bare

Grazed

Grazed,
Untold
Ships of discovery -
Light is deathless
In the pale
Dreams of birds,
Floating across the horizon,
Passed Vermeer,
Passed sky,
Through
A gentle tear
In the world.

The Burning Cup

You passed
With pale hands
The burning cup
To me.
I am hidden,
A bird of myth
Shot in the rain,
Wounded in the sky.
The sun's hand reached low
And grasped my palm
As I circled in a painful arc
And lifted my spirit
From the groundless ground
Where pain stood
And disappeared

Cassandra

Cassandra gazed
Back at me
Through centuries
Of hidden rain,
Her hands lost
In the mirror of the sun,
Her secrets unquenched
And folded into the letters
Of her eyelids,
Burning in the black ether
Of her dark points:
Diamonds
Which scorch and penetrate
The unsuspecting rhymes
Of a young
Bull
In a forgotten paradise

A King

Jesus came in softened blue,
A sire of blackened shades,
A king
With a crown
Of deep meadow
In a harvest young and strong,
In a tale
Old and deep,
In a rain
Of pale gold light
Flooding the immortal.
Sire of shadows, falconer of myth,
Sail into
Eyes
Whose pupils know the dawn,
Singing in the deep
Of Christ who married Russia
In the blood of Pentecost -
The icon shone
In shales of dark,
In the flight of mercury
And ageless hands
Whilst the hunter slept
With spears of night,
Which gathered into rings
And fell upon the earth
In the blue wind of morning

Crypt

God's hidden mirror
Has cindered the shadow
With morning rain.
Fire elemental
Strokes the emerald banner
And shaled, shimmering
Pale golds of thunder
Awaken the crypt
Of coming light;
A morning soaked
In changing shades
And the myths of the ethereal.
Rise song!
Rise beyond shadow,
Escape into the wandering blue
And discover your heart!

Breath

Veronese is a drum
Of rolling light
Flying in oceans of shimmering breeze
With the breath of
Hellenic thunder,
Freed from the icon's hands,
Written into
Light, concealed
In the shining banners
Of limbs,
Played into emerald shadows;
Roll, thunder
Into the night,
Roll into the blue
And pale gold drums
Beating
In Italian skies

Arcadian Silver

We are silent before the gods
Of the Italian masters;
Like trees we are
Quietly filled
With the stories
Of Renaissance birds,
Which perch upon our limbs
In breaths of Arcadian silver
We gently sway before their columns
Which fade into the gloom
And which pause at the junction
Of Jesus' shadowed hands

The world reawakens
In the soft shimmering breeze
Of Veronese
And the shaling gold of Titian,
Which ripples through the canopy
And wanders amongst our foliage

Streaming reds grape
Doric heavens
And thunder rolls in pale gold arches splendid
The mouth of heaven opens
And the Renaissance feeds our young
With the wine of youth undying
There can be no despair
Amidst the feast of San Sebastian
Or the Wedding Feast of Cana,

For here in cyclic splendour music re-awakens
And opens Italian skies
To our incredulous, astonished eyes -

The music of Emperors
And the dogs of courtship
Sleep in the vermillion haze -
Jugs of embroidered cloth
Sail with the mandolin
Where do you wish to go?
The Italians have countered sin!

No more darks,
Roll into the light,
Feel the breeze of Botticelli
In daVinci's deft sfumato,
Where thunder rolls
In Saint Anne's gaze
And spreads through a shivered timbre
Of unequaled meter,
In a merging of the hells
Through heaven's smile,
Into the world beyond Saint John
Whose head rejoins, in a miracle, his shoulders
In the infancy of southern fantasy -

Upon this miracle we grow
In the rain of deep El Greco,
A child of Titian and the blazing icon
Whose blue lightning
Grazes our silver limbs

Having arched from the Italian code,
Written in the ageless sky
Of Michelangelo's thunderous grace
And which now splits in the flight
Of stories from the trees

A bird
From Pygmallion's hand
Is given wings to grow
Beyond death
And into the sun
Of this marble-struck magnificence.

The Artists' Union

Is there a union for artists?
Try the builders' union
Or the maritime union
Or the teachers' union.
I looked in the waste bin
And saw a crumpled sketch
From a daydreaming hand
Of a union for artists

Black Rain

A coven of unrelated steps
Types a message
From those
Who walk
On lines,
Who walk
On concrete,
In strides dissembled
In the black rain
Of Lost,
Of Unknown,
Of forsaken rhythms
Which orbit the spiraling planets
Without the hope
Of speech,
Only shadows, shadows, shadows...

Porcelain

The porcelain president
Sits on a chair of light.
On the table is a box,
In the box a cigar
Rolled by the hands
Of Cuba.
Inside the cigar is tobacco
Grown in the anonymous shadow
Of the president's wall.
At four in the morning
The first bombs fall
Guided with precision
To depart young Ibrahim from life.
He was four years old,
Born at four in the morning
(So his grandmother told him),
Born on the anniversary of his departure,
As a billow of smoke
Rose to the ceiling

Time Unending

Expectation sits
In the soft light.
The banshee descends
As the throat songs
Of fridges rise
Declaring in deep trumpet speech
The arrival of darkness.
The banshee rises and falls,
The throat song ascends,
Power clips the hands of a coming drum.
The footsteps of music are growing in my hands
As doors swing and voices arc,
Opening and closing
Voices which drift and catch
The last lights of their cigarettes
Covered in a storm of prayers,
Furrowing into the night,
Into the layers,
Deeper deeper -

Hallowed rings of blackened gold
Upon sore toes of withered cold,

Drained of life,
Cut into the shadows,
Framed in the doorway
Of distant meadows
Where a horse chewed slowly,
Where time stood waiting

In deeper silences circling,
In closing arcs
Around the past
And through the corridor
Of dogs in stillness,
Their ears disappearing, dissolving
Onto stilts of nothingness,
Into spaceless space,
Roaming into atoms,
Lost in the junctions
Of time unending

Scales

Fire is a curtain of sunlight
Which breathes on the dawn.
An interminable hostage
Is the river bank
Which yields in a breathless gasp
To the fingers of heat,
Tearing through the curtains
To catch a glimpse
Of her sultry beauty,
The nakedness of her limbs
Forever sleeping
In the coiled waist
Of the tiger snake of the sun;
A circle of glinting scales
Refracting dark poisonous beams
Of heraldless eyes,
Born for the becoming of ancient queens
Who undulate unflinching
Through the mythical bush,
Through the fires of her hair
Which stream
In anonymous pageants of posthumous suns,
Caressing the air
Of memories, deep in the bronze quail
Of unwritten sunsets,
The blazing tails
Of revolving blue dragons
Which sweep along fractured horizons,

Of eyes
Dissembled, recompelled, and flooded
With the stories of remains,
Compressed into the bones
Of this mute and waiting
Earth

Lost Ash

Your eyes gave birth
To lights unbidden,
To black suns revolving
In the spears of night,
Holding evolution's hands
In a fathomless disguise,
Burning in hidden spirals
The lost ash
Of the unawoken,
The babes of darkness
Sketched in the pencil
Of the city
Of mysterious arrangement;
The mountain of hidden fires
Where Padron sleeps,
Where Dante turns
In ever loosening eyes,
Watching in a lidless dream
Tolkien's scared humanity
And the showers of pale gold rain
Which shale the outcrops
Of Vesas' hidden thunder.

Temples of dreams,
Humility's curse,
The wound bible of Abraham
In a coil of flight
Strikes the road
Of Damascus' saints

With its pitch of God scented tar
To pave warm blood from the jar
Of holiness, which treads
Lost and stumbling
Away from the mountain,
Away from the treasure
Where sleeps the dragon
Who protects the women
Within his scales,
Within his mirrors,
Inside his eyes
Which revolve in the limitless skies
Of blackened suns
And words which disappear
In measures
Burnt,
Lost
And cindered,
Forever cindered
And glowing.

Spears ring in the mirrors.
We stand in their reflections:
Mimes of agency,
With gifts of urgent beams
We row through silver
And into the flesh
With cries which awaken the earth
Under a softly burning sun

Speech of Darkness

The deep blue islands of the sky
Float into the speech of darkness
Nestled in the white ring
Of the summer moon.
Shadows dance on the pavement
In a sparkle of dizzy tongues:
Jewels from the ether
Refracting through the parade of wanton glamour.
The trees have hushed and the car lights probe
Voices waft like smoke
The palace opens and closes its doors
In mysterious splendour.
The eyes of all,
The palace,
The flood of the spirit,
The music of eyes
Rippling through palatial chambers
From lights to darks
In a frozen map invisble
To the clinking of glasses and the laughter which re-
lieves
And which covers
The mind of revolving chambers,
Of accidental hints
And the swoop of the birds of darkness
Below the ears of the heart

The Sepulchre of Fire

Art is mute,
Cadaverous
As a shell walking
Across the earth,
As an onyx
With bronze coins
Reserved for eyes,
Clipped in space
Behind the dark draft,
Through the revolving doors
Of sockets circulating spirit
And poisonous beams
Of snake-scaled night.

Coiled arbiters shift through the walls
The enemy has always been here
The walls have never disappeared.
Fragrant scents linger in the doorways
Roses bloom under the stair well
You might as well disappear.
The clock is ticking
But the ancient management stands firm:

Rose buds must die on the stairs

The sepulchre of fire
Leans towards music
And the piano
Sitting on the edge of time

In the unadorned lobby of Lucifer's halls
Plays a deadly hymn
Of nightshade and romance
In respect to the visitors
Who adore flame,
Who wander as shells
In the coat of the onyx
With bronze coined eyes,
And who call to the fires of Abraham
For a dance of disharmony, for a dance in hell
Through the chimera of revolving doors
And mirrors
Of magical splendour

Corridors Of Light

Corridors of light
Open in the ancient tongue,
Steps of madness glow in supine measure.
A plough in the wilderness of space
Is furrowing the hidden star,
Planting its silver music
In the soil of atomic hair.
Love burns in the clap
Of distant songs and streaming fires of gold,
Flaring through the deep corridors
Of the fathomless void.
The temperature soars as love awakens
In solar harmonies
Breathless and pure,
Burning with the violent music
Of Abraham's sons,
Flooding the temples of Matisse
In radiant colour,
In fearsome delight
With spears of sorrow
Cloaked in night
And flowers which bloom
In the star's blue hair
Furrowed and blessed

Scaling Thunder

Scaling thunder,
The dragons of sunrise,
Mute,
Unchanging,
Birthing gold
In the limitless mirrored dance,
Fracturing heaven,
Dissembling the dark,
Unfolding space for the first time
In the unimaginable parade
Of first openings,
Searing clouds into golden showers
Of unheralded light,
The mythic burns of vagrant disharmonies
Splashing in the ether
With uncontaminated joy.
Flights of angels,
Rhapsodies of tireless airs,
The flare of midnight,
The ground song of birth
Erupting in the mountain horns
Of Tibetan rites,
Through the colours of glorious thankas
Painted on the wind,
Through the swelling sun,
Flying in the circle of dragons' tails,
Streaming in pale surrender
Upon Giotto blue,
And masking

The dark lords of dance
Veiled in the coven of the secret sky:
Blades of horned beauty
Shining in the deep
Rembrandtian glade of fathomless dark,
Hidden in the wings of solar rivers
Which awaken, which burst
Into blue violins
Of deep, unquenchable love

Feathers Fell

In the darkness,
Upon the snow
Invisible feathers fell.
The midnight gown of the ancient sky
Swirled in a heapless mass.
Blue feathers grew in Rublëv's hands
In a code of solace
Which whispered from an age of bells
And echoed through the palace,
Forming stones
Of hidden words
Vibrant in the future.
A rake of fingers
Ploughed
Through the cold snows of time,
Freezing at the gates of heaven
And the gates of hell.
The unlocked icicles of the past
Speared through human memory
And blazed on entrance to the earth
With the power of Gabriel
And the fishermen of ice,
A coven of sacred doves
Who fell
Into mystery

Death Rows

Death rows
Through seamless chambers
A case, limitless and open
As the stairwell
In Babel's tower
As the oar
Dipped in Chekhov's river
With sounds of distant celebration
And stories which glide like fish
Through the cold, untraveled ether
Braced in the cool wind of Chagall's thousand suns
Temples of unbridled midnight
Shiver in the spit
Of hallowed darknesses and truth sublime
Shining gods of winter hold
The eyes of mercury
The sister of salvation's pleasure
Dining in the halls of blood sprinkled in a measure
Of constancy
Of weight
Of flutes of songs held upon the wind
Gathering the hounds of life
To grow
To play
In arcs of sensual being
Around the gathering and around the storm
Where in lies the tree
Of human eyes -
Vision's beam, lost, forlorn, passed memory and hope
Of kindling into flame

Gift

Lost in the black
Unending rain
Of pale gold thunder
Looking through temptation's purse
And finding
A gift of beads
For Mario
Forgotten in January's fires

Bitch Jazz

Are these stars real?
Myth's furled hand
What does it conceal?
Reality's timbre
Knows the hidden measure
Of my blades of grass
Light has tumbled down
And fed the sullen weed
Green are the eyes of
Nature's laughing onyx
No, I won't surrender
To Reality's bitch
The onyx is faster and brighter in pitch
He travels on rails of night
And tunes the shadows
Of ashen graves
A herald of empty light
A servant of compassless illusion

The Music of Rain

Rain is the voyager
Of crossroads
Swept in thoughtless winds
Cascading into airs
And streaming from pylons in the cold
Its touch is the element
Of cold burning silver
A message lost and hidden
As beads of aimless eternity
Born in an instant of dying mass
A grave of floating light sparkling in the air
Catching notes from the solar veil
In the music of grey English Lowry
The soft Breughel of industry and concrete
Steps splay new mirrors on the path
Trapdoors of illusion's passage
The glint of the Narcissi
Broken in the haste of mechanical conventions
But peered into by the playful eyes
Of children
The same children who played in Breughel's time
In Lowry's field of vision
And who play now in puddles of stammering division
Hands are grasped
And the mirror fades
Rain re-enters the equation
In the solace of its silent bells In the ringing
Of its soft grey palms
Let it come

Let the music of rain
Come
In quavers soft and light
To fall upon the river
And dance within the shell
Of an upturned palm
Gathering mysteries into a pool

The Prince

Machiavelli's Prince
Has strayed into the rain
A wolf of porcelain
Marching in the shade
In the guise of a martyr
Head bowed in mock sorrow;
My apologies to the wolf
In America's wilderness
For be-knighting you in a human play
To shift the pieces in a game of blood
Let us now leave you to the peace of your mountains.
The Prince is rowing through a mass of silver bodies
Human fish gleaming in a river of dumped darkness
An eye rolls, an arm twitches, like branches and insects
Upon quiet summer streams
An invasion of saints hover like dragonflies
Above the bewitching mirror
As the Prince rows he closes his eyes
And sees in the sun of his hidden gaze
The child with wounds of softened fury
Yes he is here, with a banquet of silver daggers
Unsheathed from Borges' ancient verse
Row, hands of shadow
Your oars will disappear and be reforged
In the meadows of starless hell
I will personally oversee the recrafting
In Lucifer's gentle workshop
So that you may row out of our world
Forever

A Circle

A circle of pyrite words simply rises
And I row into the river of song
A river without compass or destination
As soft Chagall once said through a painting,
It is without banks, this river of time.
Relax, rest in the shade
Attar's birds have flown too long
Through storms of darkness
They have prayed with Samuel's albatross
In prayers of flight,
And hidden sun in their glowing wings
To guide the ships below
Let them rest, let them swallow words of warmth
From crystal glasses
Let wine flow in their hearts
But the ships have no anchor in this river,
bottomless and vast
Where shall they go if you fade?
Into nothingness they will go
And you with them

Black Flowers

I feared the night would end
I feared departure
I feared the strangeness of the timbre
In the lucid hounds of song
I feared the criminals of the darkness
Rising in a black mass
Of senseless notes
So I prayed to the Hebrew god
To a mirror shining in the night
To the passing of the seraphim
With the hidden equation of notes laid bare
On the bed of the Divine Question
To answer fear
Darkness fumed from the reflection
The sound of harmonies grew dim
Eyes of warmth floated in the ether
And the promise of black flowers
Bloomed inside

A Wasp

Laced in a boot of light
Miro, unequaled by any other
Let fly his invisible swallows
Above the distant farm of childhood
From an aerial field of blue Miro
Set free an arc of wine
Flooding the sky with black suns
And vermillion moons
Tracing with molten quavers
The inflected movements of a sponge
With his hand of burning colours
A wasp in the silver darkness

Eros

Alone in the ash
Of circling splendours,
The grey doves of the nuclear eye
Fade into mirror's passage;
Flowers flood in a silver implosion
Sparkling in the wilderness
Through tales of love
Leaping in limbs of surrender
Rowing into night's pelvis
Between soft towers
In a speech of soft skinned magic
Opening
The fluids of mystery
The fluids of an unknown world
The tributaries of Eros
Night's protagonist
And the basket carrier of fruits surrendered
In the first implosions
Upon the river of bright starred morning
Which grows in breaths awakened
In the hinterlands of nimble caresses
With messages of limbs
Half aware
As two streams of subconscious -
Of a kiss placed with care
On the crevice of the unspoken
The lids of dark mirrors
Closing
In the deep blue rose

Of unceasing
To hold the soft limbed morning
In empty arms
Alone
In the circling ash
Of the eye
Fading
And brightening
A plant in a corridor
Of cold light
Offering beams of never
Of always
In hands bristling and diminishing,
Eternally proclaimed
In deathless unions
In the carriage of
Discordant harmonies
Passed into another
And another;
In a spiral of selves
Passing
Into the song
And weave
Of Eros

The Fruit Sellers

They awaken with the dawn
Slowly, imperceptibly,
Rising out of darkness
Choirs of ageless apples
Velvet songs of peach
Fruits of soft notation
Filmed in Dovshenko's *Earth*
Painted in quiet eternity by Paul Gauguin
And shifted by the anonymous hands
Of the fruit sellers who rise
Suddenly out of the night
With the strobe of fluorescent awakening
A ritual of palettes which trundle
Into and out of
My vague and transitory dreams
In a circle of suns
Emerging
In a cast of eyeless fire

Cast

Your hands are ready
To enter the workshop
The ground purrs
With the mechanical lynx
On tracks of quartz linted tar
Voices rise
Inflections from endless rehearsals
Shadows play within the tower
Cast from beams of soft pale light
Brushing opalescent
Washes upon the floor
Blue gods are hiding within the light
Vivaldi's violins are lining up in rows
One hand moves and the others follow
In a ripple of music
Gentle in the wind, sonorous in the glow
A grave of beams
Quavering in the morning song
Mussorzky's trolleys trail
The Banshee accelerates in pitch
And the wound up bird of day
Rises into the air
Solar notations glint
Off the beak
Of Murakami's bird
Singing from the well of the human void
Disciples of shade
Hunger from the dark
Speeches of sombre union

Flare in the breeze of myth
The marriage of Munch with shadow
Casts a spell of love
Dissolved
In lips parting
Through the softened hair of lovers' games
Trembling in the snow of Booth's hollow eyes
Parting where the lovers go
In a moment of surprise

Alizarin Shadow

Diversions of sunset:
Viridian hoops arcing into alizarin shadow
Bodies, conquests of gold
Questioned in the chamber
Of forgotten sorrow
A pale blue meniscus taps skin below
In a hybrid dream where cats follow
And mirrors dance
The walls are solid resin
Against the mountains of streaming light
Rivers run through hands of ice and gulp the heady flow
A mother and a daughter wade naked in the river
Their breasts shiver in the breeze
The water causes them to gasp
And laugh
As the sun rows into heaven
Casting beams of silver shadow past the mountain conifers
Awakening the mysteries of birds
Hidden in the deep-treed night
Striking awareness in limbs touched by sun
A black dog lying on the bank
Dreams of Balthus in his castle
And the pulse of nocturnal rites
Delight is the chamber of anonymous presence
As bodies dry golden in the blue
Charon's boat sails in a distant star
Life is an impregnable fortress of morning warmth
Summer's mountain, a rose of pale blue ether
To be parted by a black petal of night

And reinstated by the violins
Which grow in the auspice
Of miraculous shadows
Holding the doves of sound
Close to the skins of trees
She rises from the water
Following her mother
A brilliance of beads sparkling in the sun
A Bavarian nymph poised
In the union
Of solar dream and the solace
Of the deep and ageless mountain
Towels and hair flick in the wind
As cats prowl in the mirrors
Jumping through hoops of medieval caresses
Splash governs a rubbed memory
Held now within cotton dresses
Laid out in the future upon rocks of wilderness
For shadows of vision to slip over
And retain the essence
Of their allusive rite,
Their single mind
Born in shade and sun

The Kingdoms of Silence

The feathered spells of the onyx glisten
On rails of soft sorrow
Night's bench of justice has been filled
With the crowding flashes of the senseless rose
Dissembled, insubstantial,
An evening of fluted emptiness.
A course of dusted light fills the pasture of the calico
A Renaissance limb glowing in the morning sun
A car of bronze is humming through an eternal circle
Without destination, signaling in the airless expanse
A dream of burning skies
A hymn of acid rain,
A gift for the vision tree, humanity's eye filled branch
Birds trace time
with points of sonic beauty
As a radio blares in the muffled keep
The musicians of the day wear masks of night
The onyx skates, the bronze car rages
Unquestioned
A mood of brick and concrete
Clapping a wall of solid determination
In an arc
Around the car from which headlights peer
An acropolis is emerging
A tale of squandered Henge
A myth of burning lights
And governless revolutions
The mad hands of oil rising from a well
And crushing the wings of snow geese

In their starless grip
The flamingoes dance a ballet in the circle of the sun
Ice breaks from the Arctic
As the solar veil waves its golden shroud
The blue peace of ageless heavens resounds
in the Nordic deep
Invisible, the soundless ocean
Welcomes the kings of frost
Into its vast and seamless gown
Anonymous lamentation rises on the wind
There is no one
No one steps
The age is broken
Was never here
The kingdoms of silence
Forged in the untold geological hymns of history,
Of mirrorless time
Un-begun
Without harvest
The portals of the cindered moon
Broken and re-crafted
Energy's remonstration
Here we dwell
In the palm of splendours unspoken
Of kingdoms blooming in ageless ice
Born and cradled in the naked void
Driving cars of bronze
On a platform of eternity

Seraphim

The river is deep
Sunless fish breathe
Through aqua chambers
A discourse of earthen trenches
Dug by nature's hands of searing water
Undulating rock
Hugging the furnace
Of solarized granite
Mystery' hedge
Climbing into the breathless blue
Where arcs the lonely hawk
On beds of thermal rise
Distant
The tale of momentary ties
Riven in the soundless air
Declarations
Floating through the deep ether
Sailing above the swans
Through pillars of night
The heart is born
In the shadow
Of the servants of peace
Ever
Beyond
Purpose
The skies of anonymous
Vermillion codes
Drained from the river
Passing

Over
Stillness
Dreamt, raised
Monumental
Pillars
Drifting
With castles of hidden light
The burnt and cindered rose of ageless discovery
Wings of the bankless river
In the slow arc of the void
Pearl laced light dreaming from their eyes
Saints
Pursuers
Arks of the Covenant
Hawks on beds of air rising
Over shadow's great harness
Escaping and wandering
Above the blue chambers
Of silver fish
Breathing
In the river
Deep and soundless
Hugging the granite walls
Which undulate through the trackless bush
An anonymous nerve of thistles praying in the wind
To absence to presence
To the light of unending confluence
Dissembling forms in the basket
Of the fresh dry grass void
Wavering in a speechless union
Signaling to nothing at all -

A cold implosion sunders the anonymous water
Limbs are pierced with ice
Brightening forgotten nervature
An exhalation expounds the surface air
Quiet streams all around
But for the splash of bronze hands
And the limbs of naked youth
Dissolving wings of frozen lead
Under the wild benediction
Of a fierce and brazen baptism
Parting the solar curtain
With a message of reunion
In the slow and sultry deep
Below where thin dragons hum
In multi eyed disguise
And glancing upon the facets
Of the coiled and rapacious snake
Beaming through worlds of myth
And nature's eclectic tongue
A channel of cool in the desert's midst
For the trees of endless fire
For the children of ceaseless wounds
To be shaded by the birds of paradise
Arcing wide in the bankless air
Above the sunless fish
Where thistles wave in surrender...

The Season of Entranced Solace

The sounds of Pärt flow over the ground
A soft wind from northern climes
Building whispers of snow
Into a circling retinue
Of notes flaked from invisible hands
The country of darkness
Folds into the blue
Choirs float from chambers
Hidden in the air
The world is breathing
Beyond the brink of wars
From lakes of ancient silver
Deep in the solar glow
A parade of creatures hunting in Finland's mist
Pärt unravels in voices of lustrous dark
Trebling under
The white wings of flautists in the air
What consolation there is
What untrammeled sorrow!
The feathers of another existence
Floating in the ether
Cooling the wolves of unchecked plunder
The icon painter, with green eyed love
Is building choirs of peace
Light is braiding from his hands
In the scent of a cool and frozen wilderness
Myth burns in the secret lens of spirit's fire
The nights are ageless
Take a hand

Write a script from heaven's edge
Pursue the mountains above the lakes
Where the fish of darkness flow
An age of entranced solace
Is circling in the wind
Cast from Pärt's un-named offering
His union with the spears of light
Cast from hidden sorrow
Painted with lines of eternal hue
Opening like the flowers of a hidden star
In the land of Grace
Night spreads its conifer blanket over the deepening earth
Fields of trembling stars flower on the plains
Bent by the winds of nowhere
Lifted and dissembled
In the sagacious rites of winter
Towers of snow are falling
In soft unceasing drifts
Temples of light are growing in the soundless ether
Naked, the world is alone
A dove in the luminous void
Carrying the child of bronze
And his wing of useless lead
Towards the mountain mysterious and vast
Towards redemption
And the ladder of fire's cool interior
With hymns of darkness deeply sung
Above the music of the harp
On the lake of ancient silver

The Glade

Row, hands of bronze
Back to the shores of earth
Where the plant sits potted
In the quiet studio.

Upon the Merri path
Stands a glade
Of young gums
Nestled on a hill

A track of earth creases through
Carrying revolving tyres
Upon their way
I am spent -

A form upon the shadow
A leaf of limbs under a filtered sun
Cradled by the grass,
The soft spears of green

Jousting with a gentle breeze
Like a teeming field of samurai
"C'mon Betty" an auburn dog is called
And trots after her mistress in a down of red

Ash blue limbs arc all around
In the distance a tabla
Strikes a wafting rhythm
Drifting, like all other sounds

Away

Moonbi's Hills

Moonbi's hills drift
Into the silent evening
With the occasional staccato barks
Of dogs circling in their yards

Smoke rises as embers die
In the shadowed glades
Beyond the cemetary

Where the young and old lie
At the speechless heads of marble
Rocks glint with the final waves
Of the descending sun

Vermillion gems
Dance in the emerald gloom
The track is still warm
As the solar breath recedes

A trail of dust -
Scuttling stones in the gathering dark
Only the stars are silver
Those lakes are far away

And the night is brilliant
With a black encoded in the dazzling tomb
Of the enchanted ether
From which falls a silver lash

Coursing in white hot surrender
Into darkness, into deep
Halls of cindered death
Where floats Charon in his boat

Through channels of speechless marble
To the epitaph of an unmarked grave
Nestled by weeds within the ribs
Of the quiet ground

Here lies a bird, desecrated and lost
A beak of the shining air
Who played Time's irreproachable score
With sonic quavers high

Until one night, in the stroke of a falling star
Charon rowed into his wings
And laid the song of air
Down, at the foot

Of Moonbi's dreaming shade
The hills of cooling charcoal
Their eyes of ashen depth
Vision's sundered ring

Which lies in wait for new found treasure
On the wings of kindled dawn

Finale

The black stallion of truth,
The cosmic horse of the deathless void
Has found me in my cave
His hooves shine softly
With the light of distant suns
Still, now upon the floor of art
He looks at me with wells of ceaseless night
Reflecting on the surface
The songs of the ageless moon
Sheets of plastic ripple in the dark
Concealing the ribs of an ocean ladder,
A construct in the deep
Where men of silence build an aquatic stable
For the harem of the stallion,
The mares of the blinding sun
Who rise on the smouldering waves
Casting blood upon the blue wine bed
And spreading a warming light
Through the deathly haze
His shining hoof steps upon the floor
Resounding softly within the gloom
You are invited to the soundless mass
To where the piano plays
On the edge of human memory
To where the grass blades joust
With the shivering breeze
And to where the child sings
In the memory of the ancient harp
Softly the stallion steps

Towards ElGreco's comet
A head of searing fire
Resting on a human's disembodied summit
His astral beard of luminous white
Prays into the stallion's mane
Of cindered space
Into the mirror the stallion steps,
The mirror of ElGreco's eyes
The book is closing
To be renamed
By the mares on the smouldering waves

A Wing

A wing of unending silver
Is ringing in the trees
A stream of dying fires
Is smouldering in the shade
Forever shall I walk with ink, paper, and burning hands
In the dim light of notation's muse
With the brothers of the psalms
A train of sorrow rising
And falling in the hills
Through ashen graves of sacred dark.
The dove is flying in the soundless ether
The child sleeps on his feathered back
Beyond dreams
Beyond the fields
Which swayed with the blood
Of Lethe's bulls
And which now wave in gold surrender
To the limitless gaze of the distant suns
The message of the wind is cool
The limbs respond in gentle motion
The age of solace gains with measure
In the stillness of Tenzin's lake
Below where her cave of snow
Shelters the palace of her spacious mind
The surface of the mirror ripples
With the sound of oars
Rowed by hands of bronze
Above the sunless fish who glide
In the chambers deep

Voices drift across the wake
From the brothers
On the morning tide of prayer
Where are you?
Where do you wish to be?
An oar, a hand of bronze,
A fish in the sunless sea...

Swedish Runes

In memory of Hans Weil (1902-1998)

Speech rinsed itself in the blue halls of Sweden
Cerulean shadows bloomed
From the frozen river
Like algae shadow covered
The cobbles of Gamla Stan,
Covered the lids of closing eyes
Which rested in the winter
Like stones of forgotten light
Bicycles rolled sullenly
In the distance of their silver limbs
Mittens braced hands which disappeared
Into their dark fingered depths
A bridge of frozen sounds
Pulsed in the limping sky
The sun's dim light gazed in an echo of its splendour
Upon the face of a fading wall
All is hidden now behind the pane of seven years of glass
Dissolving slowly in the softened blaze
Of the poem's quiet lens
Through the drift a figure walks upon the silent air
Shadows climb and sing
Within the stones of the old cathedral
Within the darkness floats the crypt
Sweden's tomb of forgotten Kings
The battle plain for blades of night
And the shafts of wintry morning
The winds of Lund swirl upon the cobblestones
The sky arches its bow of gentle rain

The frozen lips of myth
Part in the approaching gloom
To whisper in the ear of shadow
Stolen from the figure walking through the drift
The shelter is as cold as ice
And I am lost in the maze of streets
Head bared and fearful in a town of hidden songs
Stumbling in the cloak of darkness
The river stares from its soft fluorescent mirror
A winding road of tinted glass
Obscured in the fuming ether
Breath is an audible scale of blue steam rising
And fingers search in the darkness for a sign of themselves
Found, lost
Black plastic ripples in the wind
Like the waves of the cindered sea
The bed of the distant mares
Wed to the horse of the streaming deep
The hour has not been sung when the blazing mares will rise
For now it is the well of the stallion's drifting lies
Which hold in the palm of Malmö
The secrets of illusion,
The anonymous poet of holographic truth
For whom language is and was and will be
"The anonymous masterpiece",
Created by all and owned by none.
The feather of his step
Walks into me
A child of wonder peeling glints
Of bird like laughter
Ruffling through the books of shelves

And pressing a promise of youth's return
Which sailed through shadows away...
I have found the street
And burn with a fever of silver keys
The palace of insoluble night
Fades in the warm interior
The corridors prove safe passage
From the mysteries of the well
Alone the lens softly burns
And steps back into the dark
Through the drift the figure steps
Blinded in the mist
Who are you?

Silence

The steps are still
A quiet voice from the inner world
Or from the drifting mist, attempts to explain:

"Firstly, please sir, would you help me across the road,
I cannot see."
Hans Weil, the inventor of the hologram,
Which he registered to the patent office in 1934,
takes my arm
We walk across the road, and then another,
Along the frozen river,
With the sun gazing down
In a pale gold echo of its splendour,
Grazing Malmö's walls with a surfeit of riches lowering
Into the grave of fading day

We walk four or five blocks;
Hans Weil probes the mystery of my arm
And raises the question of my occupation:
"Artist", I reply. "Ah..."
The inventor is light with laughter, giddy as a bird,
As we come to his apartment
Dim, and full of dust coating the sheeves of books,
The interior breathes the air of the final ark of philosophy
An island in the mist of memory
We have tea and Hans shows me an invention
Which magnifies letters for his failing eyes,
So that still he may read,
So that still the winds may turn
The bronze art coins of his perception
Cob web - like sculptures dream upon some shelves,
Poetry is the wing of his bird-like speech
And his disappointment as he must descend
To the ground of my feeble understanding.
"Come back to visit, make sure you do"
A promise broken
This poem a token for a king
And his alchemy of sorrow
Resting now in Sweden's
Blue, cerulean halls...

The Spears Of Helios

Could anything on earth
Approach the gentle braids of Homer
His dreams of fading light
Falling upon Hellenic columns splendid ?
The Muse laid her canopy of ancient spears
In a row for the bard to lift
And cast into the waiting heart of human struggle.
His wound of light opened a river of ageless silver
A pavement of moonlight spread
Through the aching arms of night
In enchantment sorrow birthed upon the river
And flowered in the darkness
With tales of truth sublime
Coursing thence through the furrowed seas,
Rising through the creases of her seamless gown
Until the manes of the stallion's mares
Flared upon the distant line of the sunless ocean
Spreading blood onto the waves
Chased by streams of gentle gold
Born of the solar mirror
In the crypt of silent space
From there the gods of Homer arched
Their bows of softened sorrow
Which rained upon the realm of men
In quavers of blazing grief
Thence the great immortals held them in the glow
Of the healing sun
Upon hammocks woven by the craft
Of the Fire God.

The balance of the anonymous void
Fed the quavers of the bard
Who sung deeply
In the quiet blaze
Of the monarch's golden halls
Now, long since the ancient spears were cast
The soft light of Homer shines
On spears laid fresh
By the ageless breath of god
Through the hands of Robert Fagles
Let us now bless and toast
His miraculous translation
Just as Odysseus acclaimed the bard,
Demodocus, of far Phaeacia

II
The Invisible Nation

The Quiet Porch

The quiet porch
In the hour of twilight
Held between the wall
And space

Inside, the fire
Outside, the prayer of grass
The spine of the fields
Rippling

In the autumn breeze.
Above, the brilliant code
Of the incandescent void
Pulsing with dark winds

Richer and deeper
Than the mountain halls of earth
The code gathers in points
Of distant flaring braille

As the night enshrouds the porch
In the secret whisper
Of forever
Music hovers

Inside the whisper
Inside my hands
A cup of distant light
Praying upon the wind

Melbourne Drifts

Melbourne drifts
Into twilight
Soft light prays within the clouds
A rosary of finch gold farewell
The road is grey
The clouds deepen in banks of dusk -
Towers of prussian blue
Sailing in the ether.
The calico is dark -
A ribbon of Veronese thunder.
The blanket of the walls
Ensigns the hermetic fate of night -
A pillow of darkness shining
For the songs resting
Upon the quiet drift of Melbourne

The Silver Moon

The black wind roams freely
Above the ice

The soft breath of stars
Sighs between the leaves

The snake of the path
Follows the seamless void

Dream is shaken
In a rustling of the trees

The midnight gown is floating
Above the mirror of song

The peddles revolve in silent grace
Slowly as the heavens

Slowly as the earth turns
On its secret arc

Hidden are the world's myths
In the soundless stream

Curious I disembark
And encounter the silver moon

Fires Yearned

Fires yearned in the deep spring
Of the calico's folds
Rippling dark winds
Filled the tips of my hands
The sunless age entered through the window
An uninvited guest
With prayers of bitten blue
I shall hold you, in any case
Bewildered bird
And calm your wings of ash
Trembling in the gloom
Smearing fire and flaring in my hands -
Surveyor of dust
Heart of a golden storm
Beat, beat the glass
And soar

A Coven

A coven of whispers
Held arms in the corner

Night remembered its kiss
Behind a pane of glass

A shift of dreaming solitaire
Held the cards of hidden night

A star appeared through the clouds
And gazed on the silver deck

Dark limned and speechless
A flare of burning braille

Reabsorbed by drifting
Fleets of mist

The night whispered on
As the rain in ecstatic order shone

Veiling the secret glances
Of the moon

Above the Stream

The dark parting of a laurel,
A river contained within
Glides across the dusted green.
A rusted iron sword is staked into the ground
A bent disclaimer rising from solid rock
A song of rust, a sentence of air and metal
Revealed within the crumbling edifice
Of what once may have been a shelter
For the stream below
And a swift conveyance for feet above
Now it is a shoe
For the lowly grazing sun
Or an eye of rock with iron lashes
Frozen like sentries at the gate
To the city of lost elements
Standing bent at the end of the war of purpose
And lit like cigarettes
By a line of fading gold -
The sun's flower closing inside it's soft ambrosia
Upon an eye of death which fades
Above the stream

Prepare

The silver lash of the street
Formed in ageless tar
Children bare their teeth
For a nocturnal smile
Horns blow indistinctly
From the radio
And my hands hover wanly
Over the verbal piano
What chords are these
Age of cement?
What coupling notes are claiming
My vision with desire?
Hot are the keys on the tips of burning hands
Slow is the breath of the night
Strung on empty whistles
Prepare
Honesty is coming
A ring of pure fire
And a marriage of light

Strange Fire

The severed whisper of snow
Lines the circle of my eye
Words are a ribbed fire
Fuming in the ether
Contracting architects
In the dark rimmed void
To unify the rays
Of the dissembled sun -
The fires of Helios
Are strung between the broken stars
Pulsing through lost sorrows
Drifting in the soundless abyss.
There is no one here
But the light
No one here
But the strange fire
Which burns on the dish
Of sovereign darkness.
Emptiness is my palm
Loss is my shadow...

Shadows Pool

The wilderness of hunted morning
Stirs in the rumbling lorry
Shadows pool like dark eyes
Under a steel grey sky
Cyclones gather to the north
Their dresses of flamenco fury
Streaming diamond rain across the drunk
And beaten earth
Eyes bloom in early autumn -
Black flowers holding emerald fires
Within their fuming mirrors
Soft ash dissembles through the city
As cloaks which drift through silent parks
A scarf of tomorrow is wound
Around the cold neck of today
Voices are sheltered.
Verbs are insignificant
From here I can only hear
A crow

Soft Wind

Soft wind hovered in space
A breath of unfurled gods
Stirred upon the ground
And rattled out in a sudden clap
Of tin
Drysdale's world creaked in the afternoon
With the pulse of dry thin air.
The starched lips of thistles
Murmured through the bush -
A nameless forgetting,
A momentary wilderness
Circling the sonic arc of the crow
And gathering shadows
Into its unblinking eye
Gaze...into the blue haven
Of the burning dome
Gaze...forever
Upon the line of the wavering earth
Peopled by rustling zyanthea
And the prayer spires
Of devoted termites
The sun dreamt
Upon the red wilderness,
A flame of forgotten cinder
Which flared in the eternal music
Of dusk
Stars unveiled their slow and distant glance
Whispering in the ether
A hall of silence opened
In the splendid sky

The tin clapped in a sudden wind
All lay still.
Stories awakened in the earth
Feet stepped through the dust
Silent
Inarticulate
Branches of lost shadows
Flickering in the moonlight
Senseless,
A warning from rock,
A magnificent archipelago of hidden words
Which remembered past embraces
Between silver light and granite,
Between limbs of soft black skin.
The fish streamed through time's bankless river,
Floating in the conquest of Never,
Gliding in the weightless union
Of disappearance,
Of sifted sand,
Of gazes ringing out,
Of palms filled with dust
Where the solace of ageless silence
Grazed and in turned
Through a spiral of mirrored loss.
Time is a temple,
Night is a palace
Of flickering lights, a harvest
Of burnt and cindered suns
Falling through hands,
Wandering through eyes
And encircling the pale dance
Of the concealed and flame-robed country

The Handflower Burns

The handflower burns;
Bells of blasphemous iron
Resound in my palm
A city of black iris fire
Encircles my pupil's rim
Everywhere vision blurs
And curtains tear
This fortune is passed.
An ache of wounded swallows
Arcs in poetry's mist
Clouds ship through
Vision's sea.
There is no resistance
A cup is lifted to cool lips
A sip of innocence closes my lids
And spreads a warm veil,
Woven by the hands of Helios,
Through my quiet limbs
Which are tensed upon the shores
Of the starlit horse,
The stallion of sunless night.
Cradles of fire are burning
In the pulsing wind
There is a stairway
Of adamantine light
Which steps itself into being.
We are steps in the curtains fire –

On the River

The floors are quiet
Outer walls drink an even light
Tight blue shadows
Grasp an iron pole
A patina of milk and dusted mauve
Dances across the face
Of a mute exterior
The world below trembles
With the purr of giant fridges
Which brace the emptiness
With sure fidelity
Rusted tin rests
Under a dome
Of ultimate blue.
A cast of accidental vision
Fills the landscape,
Primed with light
And shifting in the puzzle
Of a drifting never
Red lines the town house -
A line of 1850s mascara
Smeared across the edge
Of a field
Of dead rose shingles.
Through eyes of brick I peer
Into an ordinary world
Veiling an extraordinary map
Of silver lines and golden harvests,
Veiling the supine darkness

Of the stallion's cold and starlit breath.
The mirror turns.
The shining spoon of day
Glints
In the sheer
Invisible union
A garden rests upon a chimney
The day is clean with music
The silver wardrobe of the future
Opens itself onto a pasture
Of cerulean blues and greens
Arcadian harmonies fill the waves of ink
The blessed sunrise of the rippling muse
Gazes from the lake of spiritual balance
A force of gilded nectar and alizarin spice,
A taste of pale blue ether
Where shine Vivaldi's violins.
Temples line the coin of the rolling gift
Imparting and departing along the dust filled road
The window flares with solar news
The road glints with quartz
And cars fly with bronze hush.
The music of dust signals
Disappearance to the sun
Haze measures the grain of coming night
And dreams in the stallion's hidden stable
Words disappear into themselves
The country roams into the folds of its mountains
No where will light remain

Braille will whisper through the sky
Blind, we shall grope
Into Nothing
On the river
Of Nothing

The Photograph

Buried in mud and fire
Pearlescent bones of porcelain
Emerge from the mud shell
Stripped of human essence
They float in solid matter
Cavorting like dolphins
In the upturned sea
Spring shivers through the wake
Of chair bones
Silence hovers like a grisaille of contentment
A finger of reclamation
A wind of salt and lifeless breezes -
Emerald dust spooned into the mouth of air.
The mud palm theatre is open upon the banks of vision
A parting veil of lens and shutter, speed and light
The weight of metal
And the mystery of a dark third eye -
A wonderment of classical change merging with the future,
As the wind floats above
Dim pearlescent ribs
Caressing corrosion into the lidless night
When the lens must open its internal fire
To stake the ground
Of images
Born in water and unrobed
In the blinking, soft red sun

Equaling Zero

Sebald rises above the earthen grave
A frost of flight conjures an arabic dawn
Gentle mutations nestle in the snow
The glove of fantasy is entered by quiet hands
In the breath of early autumn
Lost grandeur prays within the sleeves of books
In echo of alpine wonders fallen
A brush caresses canvas to know failed light
To be frozen in the message of soft oil;
The tragedian's quest, nostalgia's somnambulant rite,
A husk of pearl burning in a distant palm.
O ash of life, wonder of cindered promise
Calculation of the heart's timber
Equaling zero
Striding towards the infinite moment of loss
A quail of dark feathers floats in the air
Conjoined aspects give birth in the hinterland
Where shadows graze from a shell
The earth at dusk flares in a golden arc
Fantasy dims, pleasure burns
The eye of chaos sleeps
The universe is a cyclops, a frozen palace
Of past imaginings
Of spirits lighting the chambers and passageways,
Lighting the candelabras of Balthusian night
Which flicker in the gentle air
Red storms shimmer in the desert
A grade of light steps onto an immense plain
And spreads through the starlit bush

Internal sovereignty beckons the palms of life
Arcadia flows with unlimited dawns
Cradled, the night empties itself
Into a starless cup of burnished darkness,
A braid of the stallion's mane washed in splendid ether -
A mirror leans towards your voice
Which trails in silver swirls across the ground
I am divided between reflection and substance
Forming in continual interpolation
I am divided, and lost in the divide,
A snail of ethereal symbols
Crossing the plate of zero and infinity

The Invisible Nation

A message of silk and silhouettes
A breeze plays with the louvers
Busses drive towards Baxter
Through a night of trepidation
Anxiety swells in the heat of South Australia
Where lives have been suspended
As if on a forgotten clothesline
To dry in the desert
An invisible nation is growing
On the shores of the eternal sun;
A nation whose flag is concrete, whose anthem is dust,
And whose songs are those of waiting
Waiting, waiting...
Within desert shadows, near the speech of an army base
Hope has filed for divorce
From the promise of Australia
The stiff lip of a small bureaucrat will not soften
Despite the chants of an equally ignored nation:
The culture of Protest.
A crucifix of silence settles upon the desert
As papers lay untouched
in a remote Canberran file
From where?
Where to?
Where now?
Anonymous shadows disguise the landscape of conscience
Our humanity is eroding in a sly and censored wind
The shadows of our absence divorce even the air
Gold coins spin in the sockets of our vision

And a whisper of loss passes through
Sighs of abandon float in regiments of the forgotten
Into the pool of governless night
The invisible nation rouses the muse
Like a slowly waking ox
Strumming chords of glowing, mysterious rage
Like waves of dying roses the protests strike the outer walls -
Invisible nations hearing the impotence of each other
Waving their shared flag of concrete -
The mute guardian of our loss.
The wardens of fear are scaling
A symphony of time
Whose management runs the stage
Of Australia's bright interior
The nation of protest flares and fades
Whilst the invisible nation remains and grows
In a secret city of nowhere
On the borders of nowhere
Alone and afraid

Cartilage

The silence of Sunday is unequaled
The press sits in its saddle
With the promise of journeys to come
The fossils of the day are speechless,
Speechless, white, and soft in the rays
Of the blue and dazzled dome.
They are the bones of insignificance,
The cartilage of conversations lost,
Murmured in the pallid autumn light
And carried away by yawns
Into the silent trees
Where bats and possums dwell.
Birds sing in the distance
Above the hush of cars
A mime of light caresses ribs of flaring silver
Shingles burn in their 1850s rouge
A dog signals its bewitchment
And the landscape wanders from shadow to shadow...
The burial ground of the air
Is housing the death of laughter
The white ash of memory
Floats on the gentle wind
All that was solid transpires to be
A wall of liquid,
A wall of blood,
Transparent and beautiful
As the glass of an old cathedral.
Memories have blinded the path,
Feet stagger in the solar rain
The trees are calling;
Lie down in the quiet sun

The Source

Shining palace of hidden light,
Silver robed in the distant void,
Pulsing with Arcadian harmonies,
You are the womb of the golden sun
Which conveys the solar wind,
Magnifying space with the breath
Of Aurora Borealis
Painting is the watch tower
For the silver beams of this forgotten,
This deep ancient source
Which is only ever known
Through the whisper of a dried leaf
On the concrete at night
Aside from this suppliant messenger
This source has faded beyond our lore,
Beyond our sight,
And yet -
A bird sings
In some unexpected hour
And dew glistens like lost diamonds in the grass
And the palace glimmers for an instant

Hieroglyphs

The grey thumb prints of clouds,
Limned with light,
Sigh into morning.
Croissants break our fast
And tea spreads warmth through my frame
Heroes burn with rage
In the fire ribbed books of Homer
Odysseus rains like blood
Into the mirror of his gaze
And the gods cannot see passed their attachments
Etched into the wall, opposite our building,
Is a cave-like drawing
A mysterious map of concrete lines
Suggesting antelope from northern climes,
Or wallabies from granite carvings,
Or the lines of Matisse
And drifting female forms -
Templates of floating limbs lost in Eros' chambers.
The gentle mountain of literature
Beckons with flaming hands
The scent of traceries formed in gold limned spirit
Lures me with its perfume
Stolen from the edge of nowhere
And smelt as if in another time
Hardly there, this mountain
A whisper of fire robed songs
Circling the plain of birth and death -
Hieroglyphs of concrete shuddering into life

The Crucifix of Silence

A thin line of metal grating metal greets the morning
Eyes of soldered bronze
Break slowly from their lids

A paper towel lies fearless upon the floor
The fruit sellers strike a pact with language
Which devolves under hammer blows and scythes,

A gift of sonic pulp for tired, waking ears.
A mountain of clothing, a printing press in wait,
The shells of cindered daylight calling for your limbs

The sun with its golden puppetry enlightens human cruelty
The silent bombs of the bureaucrat's pen
Detonate the tortured heart

Australia, your silence is a crucifix!
Your Christ a family of sorrows -

Condemned in the forgotten city
To feed on shadows of spiritual negation
Growing in beds of desert concrete

Like flowers of grey, unbending life
The numbers of the nameless rise
Behind fences of shining steel

Australia, your silence is a crucifix!
Your Christ a family of sorrows -

News of abuse floats on the damaged breeze
From secret desert bunkers
Upon morning songs of dust

"Rape" scorches the ears of protest
Like metal grating metal -
The sodomy of concrete with the sun

Australia, your silence is a crucifix!
Your Christ a family of sorrows -

What do you tell your children,
Bureaucrats of the blind?
Of other children locked in misery?

Or nothing, for fear of your child's gaze
Haunting you in the future,
Quiet as a tomb?

Australia, your silence is a crucifix!
Your Christ a desert shadow -

Invisible and blind the nation searches for itself
As if in a glove of endless darkness
Groping for a sign of its existence

From the castle of Fear flies the flag of negation
Rippling in the eyeless void
From which gasps...Nothing -

Australia, your silence is lost
Your Christ buried in the sun

Australia, your silence is lost
Your Christ buried in the silence

Australia,

Your silence is calling you

Speech is a Tongue of Branches

Speech is a tongue of branches
Lost in seamless fire,
Concealed in desert bunkers
And buried in ancient granite

The fire of the sky is lit
By the black crow's answer
The shining blue plate is christened
By its feathered arc

The silence stretches
In mute solidarity with the sky -
An arm of breathless blue
With veins of choking dust

Speech is a tongue of branches
Lost in seamless fire,
Concealed in desert bunkers
And buried in ancient granite

The answer circles
In spirals of the forgotten
In ribs of thin bone air
And the cartilage of our loss

Feathering from the death of words
The crow answers in sonic braille
A king of the anonymous,
A sire of the hidden void

Speech is a tongue of branches
Lost in seamless fire,
Concealed in desert bunkers
And buried in ancient granite

The crow flares with the nameless,
Colludes with desert shadows
And flies in silence
With the armies of the blind

Braille floats into the skeleton of the past
Where is built the suffering cathedral of the present
A baroque hall of Calatravan ribs
Wherein huddle the mute, the forgotten, divorced from life

Speech is a tongue of branches
Lost in seamless fire,
Concealed in desert bunkers
And buried in ancient granite

Prophesy is a beam of sunlight,
Wordlessness a thirst for life
Australia's flag of concrete echoes
With thoughtlessness, the answer of the crow

The mystery of sonic braille
Returns to its sharp winged source
Without acknowledgment, without reception,
The blank page of a forgotten song

Speech is a tongue of branches
Lost in seamless fire,
Concealed in desert bunkers
And buried in ancient granite

The lust of fire dreams
Through oxygen and solar rage
Consuming the tongues of branches
And scorching the guardians of the stars

Whispering in pale lichen
to the ears of the ageless heavens
The guardians of granite sit,
with flags of concrete, in the bunkers of eternal night

Speech is a tongue of branches
Lost in seamless fire,
Concealed in desert bunkers
And buried in ancient granite

Human spires ascend in the speechless desert
A Christian clock falls through hidden space
The Joker, Time, plays in the thoughtless sand
And the family of soil weeps in the dissembled room

The crow has flown beyond our vision,
The scaffolds of language are in place;
We must build, for good or ill the cathedral of the present
With the ribs of our resistance, the bones of endless courage

Speech is a tongue of branches
Lost in seamless fire,
Concealed in desert bunkers
And buried in ancient granite

Build, dissemble; reach, retract,
Language is falling
The cathedral is fading
Only broken promises remain

Only broken promises
And the whisper of our regret
Which dies in the fading arc
Of the black winged crow

Speech is a tongue of branches
Lost in seamless fire,
Concealed in desert bunkers
And buried in ancient granite

Speech is a tongue of branches
Lost in seamless fire

Speech is a tongue of branches

Speech is lost in seamless fire

Speech is lost...

Speech is...lost

Walls, Always Walls

Walls, always walls
Rising
Walls
Rising
Always walls, always
Rising
Always
Rising
Walls, always walls

The ladder of death
Shines like a black seagull
It floats from the clouds
Of the beyond

Walls, always walls
Rising
Walls
Rising
Always walls, always
Rising
Always
Rising
Walls, always walls

Ballad of the Lost Songs

For Schappelle Corby

The idling truck of morning
Shudders into stillness
Books wake slowly from their ranks
Stretching their spines

In the dim April glare
The leaves of my plant have risen
Like the arms of a ballerina
From a soaking overnight

The screeching banshee leans closer
Into its hideous song
And voices punch the air
Amidst the labyrinth of fruit below

Where are the songs, stolen by dreams in the night?
Where are the songs, arrested without cause?
Where are the songs, of Bali's prisons?
Where are the songs, bereft of hope?

I am calling for the songs,
For the lost ships of life,
For the abducted choirs of language
Frozen in thoughtless bonds,

Embraced by cold and brutal silence
Held by hunger in cells of sadness
By reflections of humanity
Tapping with soft insanity

Clicking their heels with hounds
Against the concrete floors of Time
Punching the nation's anthem
Upon its anonymous flag

Where are the songs, stolen by dreams in the night?
Where are the songs, arrested without cause?
Where are the songs, of Bali's prisons?
Where are the songs, bereft of hope?

I am calling for the songs,
For the whispers of the broken ships
Which unfurl their sails no more
Their good keels snapped by human hands

Upon floors which bleed through months of darkness
Soaking the invisible nation's flag
With the stains of Turin's shroud,
Whose God steps sadly through our time;

He never did leave: the crucifix always rises
Behind the walls of secret prisons
Where Plato's shadows play in endless repetitions,
Dancing with the fire, tireless in its flame

Where are the songs, stolen by dreams in the night?
Where are the songs, arrested without cause?
Where are the songs, of Bali's prisons?
Where are the songs, bereft of hope?

I am calling for the songs,
For the ballads of the ancient hearth,
For the shield of icons, deathless and strong,
To outshine the darkness of despair

May the shield's light glaze your eyes
with films of inner gold
O daughter of our nation
And like the Minotaur, lead you from the darkness

Into the clear reflection
Of Far' ud-Din Attar's Mountain
Where the songs of the sacred trinity
Rise in limitless evocation of ever increasing growth

Where are the songs, stolen by dreams in the night?
Where are the songs, arrested without cause?
Where are the songs, of Bali's prisons?
Where are the songs, bereft of hope?

I am calling for the songs,
For the ships of silver beams
Hauled up by the glowing moon
through whispers of mortal sadness,

Through the quiet, deft sfumato
Of DaVinci's peerless gaze,
Fusing poles of malice and stealthy adoration
In spells of midnight ocean spray

Where are you, songs of broken light,
Hidden in cloaks of lamentation,

Birthed in blackened charcoal breezes,
And flaming through the death of Time?

Where are the songs, stolen by dreams in the night?
Where are the songs, arrested without cause?
Where are the songs, of Bali's prisons?
Where are the songs, bereft of hope?

I am calling for the songs,
For their swift and sure return,
But they will not come; their keels are broken,
Their golden melodies are lost

Lift your frame, invisible nation,
Rise from the ground of your weeping soil
Recover your voices in songs of grief
Rally to the charge of your stolen lives

Lift and grow into the mountain's reflection,
Become like the moon's ancient white hand
Row the lost ships back to our shores
Where our daughter maybe reborn

Where are the songs, stolen by dreams in the night?
Where are the songs, arrested without cause?
Where are the songs, of Bali's prisons?
Where are the songs, bereft of hope?

A sheet of paper gleams on the table
Within its ribs, the wings of the albatross
Which hovers above the broken ships,
Frozen like a statue, static in mid air

It was carved by young Cassandra,
Given life by the Mariner's Muse,
Its ancestors, the prows of Ithaca,
Guides of blue veined marble, lost to human sight

And so the shroud of lamentation
Floats quietly to the ground,
Its gift of vision forever hidden
Above limbs which know despair

Where are the songs, stolen by dreams in the night?
Where are the songs, arrested without cause?
Where are the songs, of Bali's prisons?
Where are the songs, bereft of hope?

Where are the songs, stolen by dreams in the night?
Where are the songs, arrested without cause?

Where are the songs, bitten from suffering?
Where are the songs, bound by human madness?

Where are the songs, concealed above the ships
In hammocks of the sealed unknown?

The songs, concealed forever in minds departed?
The songs, concealed forever

The songs of our daughter,

Schappelle?

The Breath

I am out of reach
They will not come
The ships are burning in the harbour
In the torch of Turner's soul

Whispering songs of sadness
Through vagrant midnight fires
Collapsing in water's sighing palm
Aglow with pearlescent frost

I am enveloped by the tongues of branches,
Scolded by the midnight fire,
And chased by absence's hunger
Through the rows of dying ships

The night has torn the parchment of existence
Into water, fire, and song;
Three hands,
And the breath of eternal longing –

The Eyes Of Heaven

With the breath of old Tmolis
The invisible nation steps
The landscape whispers in its stillness -
Its ears of dust
Listen to the ageless passing
Of furtive cars
Dreaming in metallic stealth
And gliding under
Distant eyes of silver

The imprisoned eyes of heaven
Control the shadows on the ground
As one eye opens
The other closes -
The tides swell
And the ice-floes break
The cars of soft robed bronze
Sigh into the void,
Their fumes of ecstatic mist
Cloud the cosmic watch
Enflaming the ancient iris of the golden sun

The ground is cold
And the sky blooms in a listless field
Archaic, old, stubborn, and lost:
The dish of the hidden stars,
The blue-berry space of freshness
Which invades the mind of emptiness
And curls upon me

Like a flower
Of hidden life
The nation steps
In the motion of old Tmolis
Bristling his mountain conifers;
The anonymous saint of presence
Who stirs the lulling wheat
Through Giaccommetti's bodies
Advancing towards non-substance,
Towards the pastures
Where shadows graze
And small suns creep
Like newts of forgotten warmth

Inviolable, the nation grows
Like the plaster of negation
In the Parisian sculptor's hands:
As people of dust
With hands of granite,
Arms of highways
And legs of cratered iron
Their eyes are the sun and moon,
Their breath the winter breeze -

They are the mortal shadows
Who step in frozen silence
Towards the infinite chain of loss
Buried in their skulls
And concealed in the violet line
Of the distant, flaring earth

They are pursuers of forgotten music
Who in death release their hold -

Like Sophocles who surrendered
To the dreams of thoughtless marigold

Life sways through the nation's pasture,
Each sway a softened lie,
A breath of self-incrimination,
A trade of stolen sounds
Whispering from ear to ear

An old man, almost blind, the nation steps
A young woman, imprisoned, the nation steps
Concrete anthems and chants of protest, the nation steps
The slow pilgrimage of growing deserts, the nation steps
Through a feathered field of lies, the nation steps
Under the blazing sun and moon, the nation steps
Upon highways of endless loss, the nation steps
With legs of cratered iron, the nation steps

Into the pit of the fathomless void
Where shine the ships
Of the spiritual sun

Prisoners Of Silence

The prisoners of silence
Do not exist
The keys of time
Have vanished

The eyes of soldered
Bronze will not
Open
The lashes
Of rusted iron
Shiver through the cell

The temperature has lowered
The sun has disappeared
Our feet touch the ground
Of ice
And limp
Towards the darkness

And limp
Towards the darkness
Through centuries
Of shadows
Biting the ankles
Of the dispossessed

The prisoners of silence
Do not exist
The keys of time
Have vanished

Voices stand within the shadows
Within the soldered eye
Lost particles of vision
Praying without breath
Feeling without hands
Stepping without ground

We do not exist
Even though our eyes burn
Even though our prayers sway
Even though we strike
The floors and walls with feet
And hands of golden death

And hands of golden death
Who deals the midnight deck
Imprinted with the stars
Which form the constellations
In whose keep Orion whispers
Songs of feathered sadness

The prisoners of silence
Do not exist
The keys of time
Have vanished

He dwels amongst us
A light within the shade;
Who feathers into silence
Which carries us slowly forward
Towards the songs of the ancient hearth
Buried in our skulls

Buried within his mind
Selflessly transhuman
The highway of his glory
Breathing through the heavens
The shroud of soft negation
Who rips in the winter wind

Who rips in the winter wind
And floats within our silence
Pulsing within our cells
Through soft flourescent hearts
Upon beds of cold cement
In tombs of airless age

The prisoners of silence
Do not exist
The keys of time
Have vanished

Bars are lit by the glow
Of the silver moon
Electric wire gleams
In the beam of Power's torch
Mambas snake through the restless trees
Poised upon the tip of frozen, lidless nights

We are not here
The semblances are gone
The shades have returned
To the skulls of waiting fire
Carried into the ether
On poles of sudden lightning

On poles of sudden lightning
We charge
Into the breath
Of El Greco's oil;
Frozen flights of myth
Burnt by hands of darkness

The prisoners of silence
Do not exist

The prisoners of silence
Limp towards the darkness

The prisoners of silence
With hands of golden death

The prisoners of silence
Who rip in the winter wind

The prisoners of silence
On poles of sudden lightning

The prisoners of silence
Do not exist

We have vanished
With the keys of time.

Lost Vision

Your tongue is sealed in the night
Your wardrobe is curtained
In the darkness
Your frocks are the sighs of trees
Which you cannot see
Your slips are the summer moons
Reflected in distant lakes
Which you cannot touch
Your bras are the whispers
Of dying fruit
Lying upon the ground
Where you cannot rest
Your blue jeans are the sky
Hidden from your view
Your tongue is sealed in the night
Your wardrobe is curtained
In the darkness
I cannot see you
I cannot see you

Vincent

Shadows form in circles
Around Vincent's
Solitary nights
Radiating behind the bars
Of stillness
Through frames of quiet fire
His eyes burn
In pulsing rays of gold
Resting within his cranium
Flooding his midnight axe
Of ancestral voices
With beams of bright becoming
Shouldering the voices
of the past
With arrangements
Of nuclear precision
In a pact of naked life

Your Voice
For Ian McBryde

Softly burns
The stillness of your voice
Softly as a rain
Of shadows
Falling upon a fire
Softly as a grave
Of floating words
Dreamt for the departed
And softly as a slow emergence
Of fresh blue lightning
Traveling between frost and flame.
Your voice is a monument
Of fallen ruins
Cast into the sea,
Absorbed into its emerald gown,
Into its quiet, fuming mass,
And disappearing into its ageless body
Of mysterious, golden loss
Your words are embers
Flaring in the darkness,
Your words are coals
Blackening the light
Your words burn softly
As new born fires
Breathing
And dying
In your palm

The Preacher

You are bound to the floating grave
Of language thick with blood

You are bound to the choir of screams
Laced in the boots of earth

You are bound to the wounded child
Walking with crimson feet

You are bound to the flute of loss
Played by Rumi's ghost

You are bound to the secret lens
Of spirit's ancient fire

You are bound forever to the hidden nation
Whose shadows disappear...

You are bound to my wild swan future
You are bound to my radiant hope

You are bound to the distant prairie
Of the burning stars

Streaming in midnight masses
Through the incandescent void

You are bound, my friend, to the ears of stillness
Which hear the sirens singing

In the concert halls of time...
And you are bound to the temple of the preacher

Who ties you to a tree
And breathes with his old man's breath

Upon your tired face, until you feel soft freedom
Awakening in your heart...

Rivers Of Sunlight

Rivers of sunlight spread through the evening
Scattering swords of shadow
Unsheathed from the mouth of Darkness:
The light swallower who re-emerges
From arabic runners
Sealed in India ink.
The dark angels of trees
Sleep within their boughs
Oblivious to the soft dance
Of rivers and swords
Knowing only bark dream and root scent
The soundless code of ant feet
And the soft watch
Of spiders poised
Upon pearlescent beams of thread.
The trees' secrets are lost
In the curve of the deep, quiet earth;
They vanish
In the slow accretion
Of soil and time
The fish of heaven
Swim through streams of silver
Scaling the magnetic ether
Through chambers cold and swift
Softly the night unfolds
And trembles into starlight.
Branches are shaken
From a sudden ascension of bats
Who fly

Into tunnels of pitch
Beyond human hearing
Possums scratch
And time wanders
Through a field of autumn leaves,
Blessed and scarred:
An old man, a young woman,
Shimmering, delighted;
Full of dance and despair,
Swirling in a cloak of autumn's fire,
His chest invisible, her eyes ablaze;
Their light undying, her hands fresh
And blooming
In fevers of uncharted unions
Hovering above
And descending upon
With the flare of intuition
And the joy of forbidden love -
Time struggles upon autumn's bed
And glances eternally
Into soft-fired heaven

Autumn Elegy

For Shelton Lea

I am defeated...again and again
I am bourne through this old pageant
Of dying shadows
Upon swords sheathed in darkness
Burning in the choirs of heaven
All wonders glow
In this interminable night
Aspirations fall
Like forgotten petals
From my hand
The ladder floats
Gleaming and soft
Braille whispers to the wind...
Silence is the spoon of eternal secrets
The night opens itself
Like a lost God
Removing our masks of emptiness,
Teaching us music
And wandering through distant fields
Where grasses ripple and flowers pray.
We are welcome,
If we are to be ears of dust,
We may listen
For the songs which are lost
For the songs which wreathe
The dying of the shades
For the songs which wreathe the crown
Of the disappearing king...

Portal

The night is a trophy of stillness
The exit sign gleams
Soft and cool
The space is empty

Beams cross the ceiling
Like the ribs of a disused ship
Pillars stand in perfect verticality
Arms outstretched
Like divers poised upon the edge

The door is a turquoise shell
Of ancestral weight
Guarding the secrets of emptiness...
Behind the door darkness sits
Like a black cloud of promise

A finger of charcoal dust
Might reveal a Rembrandt
Encrusted in the gloom
Or an icon, pulsing with inner heat

Behind the turquoise shell
Is a lost world
A portal which beckons
The agitated soul
Towards harmony, towards detachment,
Towards the cindered rose
Of fresh discovery...

Ever

I am touched
The silence hovers
Inside the dim light
Like a flower of peace
Opened for no purpose,
For no one.
Its petals
Are the breath of Time
Awakening
Born
And bathed
Upon the lip
Of Nothing
A slip
A discordant message
A meteorite
Without meaning;
Handflower, starfield
Time watch;
A casement of yearning
Upon the bed
Made
Untouched
Empty
Of feeling
Devoid
Of necessity
Open
Yet closed

An un-needed aid
In the quest for the field
Dancing upon the edge
Of the twilit house
Unreal   forming
A gown   of walls unbroken   unmade
Ready for the breath   of Ever -

Beyond The Walls

Crisp hands stroke the morning
Icy feet
Step into autumn's gown
The day is clear
The light through the window - sharp
Pigeons bathe in the sun
Their claws curl around steel
poles of blue indifference
In packs of thoughtless knowledge.
The eye burns slowly in the wide expanse
Red brick glares coldly
Under its
Breathless beam
Whistles encode the secrets
Of winged nature:
Birds in the night are born in a bell.
The cassowary dreams on acres of earth
Near
Where the dam lies
Beyond the field
Within the gully
Outside the radius of monastic chants
Inside a monastery of leaves and trunks
Old and webbed
With the luminous parlance
Of arachnid courts
And the dampening crush
Of morning rain:
Stillness -

The light balance of worlds
Rests upon an outcrop
Of green-moss rock
Where the cassowary beams
From beyond the walls of indifference

Silence

Silence.
Darkness rests like a cloud
Upon the whispering streets
It plays through the parks
Like an invisible child.
Possums crawl and rise
Like sudden tombstones
Before rushing up gentle trees.
Cars hush in their rhythm of bronze
Tracing paths beyond darknesses, beyond lights
They groom and are gone.
Emptiness sits
Like a flower of cherished doom
It sits inside, like a silver dream.
It sits behind a turquoise door
Soldered into the chasm.
The door is strange
And belongs to darkness.

I am here, a finger of dust
A pause of heat, moving through the chamber
Tracing its stillness

The silence is a monolith of lost dreams
A tide of mouths
Fallen
Tongues of shadow
Treasures of the chamber.
There is no sound
Air has lost its movement.
I am a tongue in the shadow
A fossicker of silence

The Chamber Grows

The depth of your knowing
Is tuned to the shadows' radiance

The chamber grows
In your quickening

An insoluble darkness
Spreads
Like the gown of pre-history

Your hands grow

The night has been swallowed
By the earth
And glimpsed
By the cold moon

Fragrant roses
Bloom along the hedge of Nowhere
For the child of lost vision
To pick and carry
Towards the image
Of the Preacher
Frozen in the Temple

III
Night Palace

River of Names

Words lay buried, deep in the silence. They are
sculptures; invisible men and women of stone,
faceless, limbless. They come to me as if in a dream.
Words. Archaic lanes of stillness. Feathers of loss
falling quietly to the ground. What ground is that?
The homeless ground. Where the sculptures live,
where the dream and language are buried. Fossicking
the dawn. Fossicking the sun. Words detecting
themselves, unveiling themselves - gods and goddesses -
strange whispers unfurling, un-naming, reforging their
masks in the quiet emptiness. It is barren. There is no
pretense. No naming where there are no names. Words
drift in the deep forgeries of the world. Blank states of
being, they curl in the fires, where they burn, before
they lift, before they rise to the Tongue of Being,
to the defeated face of Meaning, to the beautiful
river of names.

The Game

He comes with flowers. He comes alone. A shadow on
the pavement. Born of sun and skin. He comes and
the wind can feel it. A passage of space breathing. A
wineskin of time receiving and releasing an inarticulate
flow. Hands. Soldered into pockets of bronze. Only the
faces pass, smile, defeated. Does any one know?
He comes with flowers and surrenders, once, then twice
to the game.

Relinquish the Snow White Bones

Shadows lay in pieces, broken. Arms lift and carry the fragments, without hands. Tomorrow is lost. Centuries ago the reliquaries stood in silence, appeasing the dead. Torches lead the pilgrims to the bones of the living. Torches lead the pilgrims through the labyrinths of Tomorrow. They flared in the silence of the golden arms which held the broken shadows. There is a song inside the gold. But first, relinquish the snow white bones flowering in the House.

The Carpet of the Living

The carpet of the living is strange. Do you trust it?

It Sang

Strange fires sang discordant notes in the halls.
Emblazoned signs appeared. Glyphs melting from sight
and into heart. Pumping blood and never tiring of the
cadence. Even though the snow discoloured. It sang and
the rain poured into the fire.

We all Pause

Cadences. Microtones of loss, of being. Small airs.
Insurgencies of sound. Break open. Hover. The sounds
are not complete. It does not matter. Somewhere the
charge begins. The bright inscriptions flare and are
forsaken. Language sips its own defeat. From a glass
swirling and darkening it sips. We all pause while the
emptiness grows. The patrons of negation sound their
armies through the mountains of the icy earth.

What I Found

Seeking solace I entered the palace and found a shining
mirror. Portrait of the centuries. Confiscated amalgam,
hieroglyph, telegram, from the ocean of the conquered,
the slain.

Seeking solace I entered the palace and found dust
drifting over frozen bodies. In place of prayers I found
fragments of darkness, glinting softly in the evening air.

Words which are Lost

I lost scent of the music. The museum stood in silence.
A chain of broken gods. A wandering pillar looking for
its temple. Do not look. What is broken is broken. You
will always be in the wrong places, floating upon the
wrong lines. Brokenness has its own air, its own keys. If
you offer to translate the page may brighten. Your song
is falling through words which are lost.

It Fell From the Dove

For Ruth

There is little. That's enough; a form which follows zero.
A quiet trespass across the boundary. What boundary is
that? The boundary of what is known. Is there any more
to it? No. Wait, a wing. It fell from the dove of Sancho's
'Holy Spirit'.

New Moons

Shadows swell with the light. My pulse harvests a new
beat from its veins. Tremours of awareness. Static plays
of verse. New moons of lines raking themselves thin as
slowly cracking ice.

He is Walking in the Hills
For David

The pale shell of autumn has ordained that you cloak
yourself in flowers. A flower forest walking with 'ghost
painting' steps carved by flourescent rays under neo-
gothic eaves. Thus Clayden's compressions walk anew
through the ancient tower of memories frozen, the
calcified remains of the Christian Passion. Abject
stains on a calico curtain, a veil of ghosts trembling,
disavowing, un-enchaining the golden light of Christ's
neo-gothic prison. He is walking in the hills. He is
praying with the birds.

The Canyon

Sentences carved in the ear travel along roads of quiet absorption. The canyon of meaning echoes echoes echoes. It strings beads of light along the thread of itself. Dying rays fill the canyon with a soundless hymn, touching particles of space with fingers of wondrous departure. The canyon is a chalice of red dust, heat, and silence. As it darkens the rim flares, a salutation of hidden light, a gift of itself, knighted with its own sword of gentle fire in a soundless benediction, un-chronicled in the library of the fathomless void, the aisles of which close, draw in, unite in a booth of oblivion and death.

Aslan

I am hidden in the brightening page. A somnambulist
of verbal snow. A warden of the invisible, along with
Aslan, Lewis' fearless lion who defends the Kingdom
which hovers - softly- beyond the border, leaving tracks
gleaming in the pallid light of a candle which flickers
above his realm at night, enchanting the souls of
innocent hearts, that they may enter their own realms
of silent transformation.

A Letter is Waiting

A letter is waiting. Within soft paper its heart is beating. Triumphantly. Distantly. A message so close in its distance. Like the paradox of a strange lover glistening in ones arms or the familiar face of the moon no one has ever known.

A letter is waiting. And the keys which form the dance hover - wordlessly, breathlessly - above the fuming expanse of possibility.

Let us Leave

In the mountain of solitude where no expectation lives the poems of others circle in cadences born for the inner mountain's air. Within this ring of finite sound memory re-enters its hidden past. A drum for the invisible. A wing for airless space. A journey into the heart where quiet resounds and the world recedes into the grain of its distant self. A grey rock held by light, a golden willow wetting its leaves. A breeze blowing over empty fields. Someone is coming with a barrow of mud for the baking of bricks and the building of rooms. Let us leave and re-enter the mountain and consider the twilight which reigns within its halls.

Trailing Evening like a Gown

I have abandoned the buildings. Clothed in sunset
I sail, trailing evening which spreads like a gown
throughout the world. I have touched the mountain
like a hand caressing silk and have left the canyon
like a child letting go of his mother's gentle grip. My
infancy is space. My cry, a beam which illuminates
the dust which travels on its shaft. My delight is your
wonder which breathes through me as through a pane
of reciprocal glass, stained like a jewel by the luminous
Middle Ages. Chartres grew like a flower in my mind,
a canopy of ageless stone held up by pillars as slim as
stalks. And filled with song which rose upon ladders
of sonic breath, scaling the hieroglyph of heaven
which unfurled its secret scent. Walk with me upon my
humble ship. Clothed in sunset I sail, trailing evening
like a gown.

Balance the Roses

Balance the roses. What is that? Balance the roses.
Again, what is that? Twins balance roses in the
darkness. In the mirrors, in the darkness. Roses shine,
balanced by the twins in the mirrors of darkness. They
are simply words and yet they grow within like a strange
fruit, like a ladder into a world of its own creation. Like
Balthus' glinting gems of vermillion or the sighing gold
which dwells in Rembrandt's oil. The roses are balanced
and the flutes of emptiness are held. By the twins in the
mirrors, in the hallways of the palace. The vision hovers
like a wafer. I am not sure it is real. And yet it flows, it
haunts. It is a part of this place which does not exist.
And yet which persists with a music both familiar and
distant. A scent of the rose. It bloomed on a page which
fell from nowhere. Now its fragrance fills my field.
A petal of spring. A satin dove of sound.

Shamans of the Page

The words are soft, familiar. They are shamans of the
page, knights of an invisible kingdom. They grow within
me. I who am Chartres, a cathedral of God, a palace
of the night, an abode of the birds who wing through
the darkness, who call in the secret chambers with
a song so distant and so achingly close, a song of
fire which dwells in my eyes and flares in my hands,
archaic, lonely and serene. The jewels of the night are
memories, gods and hymns which pulse from the lip
of nowhere. Hidden staircase of the sublime, steps of
light polished like stars, feel this breeze which flows,
an air of unconquered sound, a flag of the human soul
raised in the magical chaos of the inscrutable void, the
unknowable tomb of loss where loss itself ceases and
where cold sorrow passes like a silent egret alone in
the wilderness of space.

A Hand of Gold

Grey palimpsest of winter. Sigh of leaves in the air.
Drawbridge of sounds lowering from the poem's gates.
Voices rush in with the chill, games cackle through the
halls, confidences slip from ear to frost-tipped ear, and
old tongues circle phrases loved like roses tended upon
meticulous lawns. Candles are lit and the voices turn to
murmuring like water trickling in a stream, glinting in
the gentle light which wavers and flares, point to point,
flickering and dreaming amidst tables covered with
dishes which steam and waft gently, un-enchaining a
banquet of aromas which drift through the voices like
invisible birds on the wing. Wine is tipped, stirred,
beheld. A solitary hand raises a toast to the guests of the
palace. The murmurers applaud and cutlery resounds
throughout the halls. The night is endless; a pageant
of shadows burning through the mirrors which shine,
absorbing the sounds and signs of numberless guests. I
retreat into the chamber where a hand of gold reaches
out and invites me to rest.

The Warmth of Life

Frost-soled night. Palatial stillness. Lost colours
floating through quiet chambers. Squares of red edged
in black. Cerulean diamonds gently pulsing. You may
enter; the palace is deep, a ship yard of frozen songs,
an ice age of verse as solid and impregnable as the
land of Pleijel's *Dead Queen*, or Lewis' snow-locked
Narnia. Inside is a treasury, an unwritten dream, a
scent of memory floating along the bow of a distant
violin. Take shape hands; hold this gentle swan, this
spirit clothed in gossamer down. She is the bird-child,
born for a moment and wounded by the light. Hold
her, quiet notes, let her breathe. The ships are silent,
the chamber gleams. Music is soldered to the wings
of this apparition, this invisible wonder which is our
connection to the warmth of life.

Wild Flowers

A lost sign is flowering on the plain. Beyond the
outskirts of meaning it flowers. Beyond the ring of
sulphur. Beyond the bronze sculpture of Paddy Hannan,
the gold miner, central to the myth. An excavator of
time, Paddy Hannan grows, into the flower of the sun
he grows. The sun which never sets, which freezes
upon the horizon, which bleeds into the line of the
earth curved with dust, curved with wind, curved with
the soft sigh of a secret breeze tousling the leaf of a
eucalypt, the hair of a grass tree, and a soft spindle of
silent spinnifex. Amidst it all my father wanders, a lost
sign upon the plain. A driver of forever born upon the
wind, carried by the vast, insoluble silence, resurrected
across the heart of the Nullabor, the ancient grove of
absence, dying in the night like a wounded dream,
flowering with the stars, rising with the first light,
ghosting the dawn. And there is my mother, shadow
upon the earth, carrying the absence upon her and
within her, shouldering the silence, accepting the
parcel of shattered glass, placing the pieces in a box of
albums and watering the desert with her quiet tears.
And there am I, a prayerful moon; and there is my sister,
a tear-filled ray; and there is my brother, a whisper of
life, a gurgling spring, a soft-skinned babe. A family
rolling through the desert, rolling through the silence,
gathering space, stifling dreams, hunting horizons of
wild-flowers, of gold, of desperate love. And finding
pyrite, ghost love and empty tanks.

THE CALL

I. Within the Deep Hall of the Night

The attraction to the chamber is strong. The light there is cool. What must you tend to? What space of inner light draws you towards it?

Silence gnaws at my heart. There all is silence, except for the courtship of iron bells. Why bells? Because they are partners with peace. Because they clarify and deepen the space within.

The space of the chamber, articulate and knowing.

The chamber is the palace of silence, of quiet infinitude, blue and magnetic. Its call is a pulse of inner strength, of interconnection with the quiet landscape.

Birds filter through the landscape. Their songs are loosed in light arcs around the trees and around the thistles and through the flowing air. The voices of the birds are born in the bells of night, when the chamber opens in secret darkness.

The call is soft and strong: a chant rising and falling in the hills. Desire is the twine of the rope which holds me, which moors me to my weakness; my weakness: the sacred I. The sacred I will hold onto the twine of Desire which is the meeting point of the world: which is the possibility of your friendship. The friendship with your equally entwined I, precious and beautiful in its aspect.

Beyond friendship, the chamber calls. And the ship longs to be released from its mooring. Will it return if it departs? Is there any return? To remain is to create in weakness. To depart is to go beyond; to be refreshed in the light of the chamber. This question is urgent to my soul, which is born with the birds in the darkness.

What is dawning within this radiant pillow, within this luminous bed? A question which floats in the promise of its soundless answer. The blue river has formed at the mouth, and the ship tugs at the twine; the twine which holds fast with thoughts: thoughts of you, naked in the twilight; thoughts of you, laughing in the sun.

A blue butterfly perches upon the crown of my head. Without reason. It is an ally of words without reason.

The blue river spreads from the mouth. I do not know where it is going. It is a river of sounds, illuminated from within.

It carries the ships of unknowing, into the dusk of the unconditioned, where the chamber glows like an ember, within the deep hall of the night.

II. Prayer is a Tide of Darkness

A tide of prayers, black as the velvet darkness, waves through the silent chamber.

The wind is soft as a bell awakens from the silence.

Its iron tone renders the landscape alive and audible. It pulses through the chamber, deepening its silence and increasing its beauty.

The memory of the iron tone is suspended in the chamber. It is suspended within the tide of prayers, which wave slowly through the darkness.

Memory and tide gently rock the static ship; the static ship moored at the mouth of the chamber, moored at the mouth, blue and magnetic. It rocks and gently tugs at the twine of its mooring.

From within the chamber another bell intones its iron song, swelling with the tide of prayers up against the static ship. Once more it fades into memory, layering upon the previous tone and dwelling within the tide.

The ship resounds with the memory of the bell, its timbers alive with its iron vibration. Now the silence deepens, the ship calms, and the blue light of the chamber grows.

The ship, anchored at the mouth of the chamber, waits. What is it waiting for? For what sign? Why has it come? Why has it been called?

The ship longs for the chamber. Aboard is a treasury of tiles; the tesserae of the secret heart. Their unwritten rhythms await. The host awaits their coming.

The rich embers of the spirit are burning within the tesserae, hidden in the hull of the static ship. The ship is moored and cannot move. The twine holds fast and the ocean is still.

The twine must break, for the host is waiting for the music of the tiles. We must let go of the mooring, whispers the ship. We must discover the darkness of the chamber and the songs of unknowing; we must come to know the limitless gaze of the spiritual sun and the frozen tear of its echo, the moon. We were made for the chamber: our songs are born within its depths. The rhythms of the burning tesserae are calling for their birth.

III. At the Mouth of the Abyss

I have boarded the ship
At the mouth of the abyss,

Its timbers humming
With the soft vibration

Of iron bells;

Bells which ring
In the unaltered abyss

And fade into silence
And dwell in the tide

Of prayers which flow
Into the darkness

Lapping the hull
Of the static ship.

I have boarded the ship
At the mouth of the abyss

A pilgrim, a pilot, an author,
Unknown;

Its timbers humming
With the soft vibration
Of iron bells,

Bells which ring
In the unaltered abyss

A cage of dreams burning
On the edge of Becoming

A cage of dreams burning
Through the maps of our knowing

Into soft ash and shadow,
Fresh loss and grace -

A ship of dazzling fires
Disrobing its songs

Upon the ocean's dark
And rippling hand.

I have boarded the ship
At the mouth of the abyss,

Its timbers now burning
In a bright conflagration

Of glowering air
And mysterious rage

A palace of flame,
A shimmering pearl,

Cracking its shell
Upon black bones of water -

Sighing into the ocean's
Bright seamless gown

A ship of white fires,
Sinking in silence,

A ship of white fires,
Collapsing in peace,

A ship of white fires,
Slowly releasing

Its dreams from its cage
Into the mouth of the abyss

Where tongues of iron
Ring in the darkness

And resound in the silence
Of the incoming tide.

IV. The Tesserae are Burning

The tesserae are burning inside the chamber. Their
rhythms awaken a shield of icons, deathless and strong.

Rivers emerge from the icons. Streams of fluid radiance
float from their blazing shield.

Language arises from the rivers: numinous particles of
speech, unmeasured, unborn.

Slowly, within the quiet mist of speech, a pilgrim wanders.
He wanders from particle to particle; a mendicant of
the chamber, a purveyor of the anonymous: a seeker
of harmony.

The pilgrim is a guest of the chamber, a composer of
light and a resident of beauty.

He is the field of the Farmer, furrowed and ready for
the sowing of seeds.

He is the Drawn of the Drawer. He is the Created of
the Creator. He is the author who dies at the mouth, blue
and magnetic.

He is the pilot of the burning ship who shines in the
realm of Death.

NOTES

Cassandra (p. 8)

According to Greek mythology Cassandra was a Trojan Priestess with the gift of prophesy who was fated never to be believed.

Lost Ash (pp. 22-23)

Justo Jorge Padrón (1943-2021) was a great Spanish poet. Tarjei Vesaas (1897-1970) is considered one of Norway's greatest writers.

The Sepulchre of Fire (pp. 25-26)

Onyx is a semi-precious black stone, which, according to crystal healers, is said to offer protection, strength, focus and willpower. The 'onyx' in 'Kingdoms of Silence' is imagined as some kind of creature, lexically converging from 'oryx', and 'lynx' as an imaginary wild cat with the protective qualities of the stone.

Feathers Fell (p. 30)

Andrei Rublëv (1360-1440) was a great Russian icon painter.

Bitch Jazz (p. 33)

The 'onyx' is affirmed here as the new voice of the poet. See also 'The Sepulchre of Fire' (pp. 25-26).

The Music of Rain (pp. 34-35)

Pieter Breughel's paintings of wintry village life coalesce in the poem with the wintry urban-industrial landscapes of the English painter L.S. Lowry (1887-1976).

The Prince (p. 36)

Niccolo Machiavelli (1469-1527) was the author of 'The Prince', essentially a treatise on power; how to take it and how to hold it. Jorge Luis Borges (1899-1986) was a great Argentinian writer and poet.

A Circle (p. 37)

"Attar's birds" refers to the agents in 'The Conference of the Birds', by Farid ud-Din Attar (1145-1221). "Samuel's albatross" refers to the albatross in Coleridge's 'The Rime of the Ancient Mariner', a guide for the mariner, out of the Antarctic ice.

The Fruit Sellers (p. 42)

Alexander Dovzhenko (1894-1956) was a Ukrainian Soviet filmaker, whose film 'Earth' is recalled in the poem for its footage of fruit, coalescing with Gauguin's paintings of the same and the author's memories.

Cast (pp. 43-44)

The "banshee" was a roller door, aparently never oiled, on the street below the author's studio, where he worked in Melbourne, 2005. Haruki Murakami (1949-) is a Japanese author, whose book 'The Wind-up Bird Chronicle' is referred to here. Booth refers to Peter Booth (1940-), an Australian/English painter, whose paintings of snow coalesces in the poem with Edvard Munch's paintings of lovers.

Alizarin Shadow (pp. 45-46)

Balthasar Klossowski de Rola, known as Balthus was a French/Polish painter, (1908-2001) whose compositions of nudes, cats and mirrors here coalesces with memories of travels in Bavaria.

The Season of Entranced Solace (pp. 52-53)

Arvo Pärt is a contemporary Estonian composer of classical and religious music. "The child of bronze" refers to the one-winged 'wounded child' figure who first appears in 'Rings of Blue' (the second part of the author's first volume, 'Insomnia's Gates'). He also appears in the poem 'Seraphim' (pp. 49-51).

Moonbi's Hills (pp. 55-56)

Moonbi is a village in north-west N.S.W. Australia where the author's family moved to when he was a teenager.

Finale (pp. 57-58)

"El Greco's comet" refers to the beard of Saint Jerome in El Greco's painting 'Saint Jerome as Scholar' (1610).

A Wing (pp. 59-60)

"Lethe's bulls" refers to the violent agents of the author's previous collection 'Blinded Bulls'. Tenzin refers to Tenzin Palmo, a Tibetan Buddhist nun, whose story became famous through her popular biography 'Cave in the Snow'.

Soft Wind (pp. 78-79)

Russell Drysdale (1912-1981) was an Australian artist known for his desolate paintings of the outback.

Equaling Zero (pp. 85-86)

W.G. Sebald (1944-2001) was a renowned German writer, whose work the author was reading at the time this poem was written. Thinking about his work became a catalyst for the main body of the poem.

The Invisible Nation (pp. 87-88)

Baxter Detention Centre was built in 2002, near Port Augusta in South Australia, to 'detain' (read: imprison) asylum seekers who arrived in Australia illegally by boat from Indonesia. It became a site of protest, both from within and without and was ultimately closed in 2007.

Ballad of the Lost Songs (pp. 100-104)

Schappelle Corby was convicted and jailed in 2005 for smuggling cannabis into Bali, a charge which she resolutely denied, claiming the cannabis must have been planted. Her trial was of the highest profile and was exhaustively covered by the Australian media. "Far' ud-Din Attar's mountain": refers to the holy mountain of Kaf in Attar's spiritual classic, 'The Conference of the Birds' (1177). "Far' ud-Din Attar" is an abbreviation, for metrical purposes, of Farid ud-Din Attar, the pen name of the Sufi author.

The Eyes of Heaven (pp. 106-108)

Tmolis refers to a mountain, personified in a tale from Ovid's Metamorphosis. "Giocometti's bodies" refers to the sculptures of Alberto Giocometti (1901-1966), imagined in the poem as personifying the Australian landscape.

It Fell from the Dove (p. 139)

"Sancho's 'Holy Spirit'" refers to a poem by Ruth Sancho Huerga, titled 'The Holy Spirit'.

He is Walking in the Hills (p. 141)

Reference is made to James Clayden's video installation, 'Ghost Paintings', which was shown as part of an exhibition in St Patrick's Cathedral, Melbourne, titled 'Crisis, Catharsis and Contemplation', curated by David Rastas in 2006.

Aslan (p. 143)

Refers to 'The Lion, the Witch and the Wardrobe' by C.S. Lewis.

The Warmth of Life (p. 150)

"Pleijel's *Dead Queen*" refers to a poem from 'Poems by Agneta Pleijel: Eyes From A Dream' . Translated by Anne Born for Forest Books 1991.

Wildflowers (p. 151)

Paddy Hannan (1840-1925) was one of the first gold diggers to find gold in an area that was subsequently founded as Kalgoorlie, a gold mining town on the edge of the Nullabor plain in outback Western Australia. It is where the author spent his childhood.

Printed in Great Britain
by Amazon